ROCK EXPLORER

GEMS

Claudia Martin

Quarto is the authority on a wide range of topics.

Quarto educates, entertains and enriches the lives of
our readers—enthusiasts and lovers of hands-on living.

www.quartoknows.com

Editor: Clare Hibbert
Designer: Dave Ball

First Published in 2017 by QED Publishing,
an imprint of The Quarto Group.
The Old Brewery, 6 Blundell Street,
London N7 9BH, United Kingdom.
T (0)20 7700 6700 F (0)20 7700 8066
www.QuartoKnows.com

A catalogue record for this book is available from the British Library.

ISBN 978-1-78493-963-2

Manufactured in Guangdong, China TT022018

9 8 7 6 5 4 3 2 1

MIX
Paper from
responsible sources
FSC® C016973
FSC
www.fsc.org

Contents

What is a Gemstone?

A gemstone is a pretty mineral or rock that is used to make jewellery.

Lemon quartz

Rose quartz

Quartz

Amethyst

Green amethyst

Citrine

Smoky quartz

MINERALS

Most gemstones are minerals. They form underground when hot, liquid rock from inside the Earth cools down.

CRYSTAL GEMS

As a mineral grows, it forms regular shapes called crystals. Only hard, beautiful minerals are used as gems.

Quartz is a hard crystal. Purple quartz is called amethyst. It is a popular gemstone. ▶

Using gemstones

Gemstones need to be hard. Nobody would buy a jewel that could easily crack!

▲ This gemstone jewellery includes amethysts, green malachite and amber.

▼ Aragonite crystals are too soft to be gemstones.

Colourful
Jewels

Some gemstones are brightly coloured.
Gems take on their colour as they form
in the ground.

Rough
ruby

RED AND BLUE

Rubies and sapphires are
both made from the same
mineral, corundum. On its
own, corundum has no
colour. But if chemical
elements mix with it,
it's a different story.

Rough
sapphire

Polished

This is a ruby. It is red
because the element
chromium got into the
crystal as it was forming.

EMERALD GREEN

An emerald is made from the mineral beryl. It is green because of tiny amounts of chromium and vanadium.

Rough emerald

Polished

Precious rock

Unlike most gemstones, lapis lazuli is a rock. Rocks are mixtures of different minerals.

Polished

▲ This is a sapphire. It is blue because iron and titanium mixed with the corundum crystal when it was forming.

Lapis lazuli is an amazing deep blue. Long ago people ground up this rock to make paint. ▶

Dazzling
Diamonds

Diamonds are the hardest minerals.
They are made deep inside the Earth.

A pure diamond
has no colour. ▶

This diamond has
not been shaped
or polished yet. ▶

PURE

Diamonds are made of the element carbon. Elements are pure materials that are the building blocks for everything on Earth. There are more than 100 elements.

Pure gold is one of the elements. ▶

ANCIENT GEM

All diamonds formed at least one billion years ago. They were made inside rocks that contained carbon. Carbon has to get extremely hot before it forms a diamond.

Sharp as a knife

Diamonds are so hard that they can cut other materials. They are used in drills for cutting rock or metal.

The tip of this drill ▲ for polishing metal is made of diamond.

Precious
Patterns

Some gemstones are prized because of their stripes, spots or other amazing patterns.

BLUE STRIPES

Agate forms in an empty pocket inside a rock. It grows slowly, layer by layer. Different colours are made as the temperature or pressure changes.

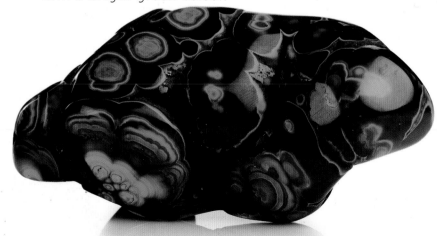

▼ Malachite is a banded mineral with a bright green colour.

Agate is made from the mineral quartz. ▶

Ball of jasper ▶

JASPER
Like agate, jasper is made from quartz. Unlike agate, jasper is opaque, which means it cannot be seen through.

▼ This spotted rock is named Dalmatian jasper, after the dog.

WILD STRIPES
Tiger's eye is a rock made of quartz and other minerals. The quartz crystals have grown in stripy rows.

Tiger's eye reflects the light like a cat's eye. ▶

Hiding
Inside

Gemstones can be hidden in surprising places – inside dull-looking stones, other gemstones and even shells!

SECRET MINERALS

On the outside, a geode looks like an ordinary rock. Break it open, and you discover crystals have grown inside!

This geode contains amethyst crystals. ▶

MINERALS INSIDE MINERALS

A mineral can grow around the crystals of another mineral.

A mineral called rutile is trapped inside these quartz crystals.

A star sapphire contains crystals of rutile that form a starlike pattern.

STICKY SAP

Amber is a clear, golden gemstone. It forms from sticky resin that oozed from trees millions of years ago.

Pacific pearls

Pearls form inside the shells of oysters or other shellfish. They are iridescent, which means they shimmer and seem to change colour.

Found in the Ground

Most gemstones are found inside rocks in the ground. They have to be dug up or blasted out.

▼ This huge emerald is from an underground mine in Colombia.

MINING

Some gemstones are close to the surface. Miners dig an open pit or hole and check the rocks for gems. Other gemstones are deep underground. Miners dig shafts and tunnels to reach them.

BOOM!
Sometimes miners blast rocks apart with big explosions.

An explosion in an open-pit diamond mine ▶

ROUGH GEMSTONES
When gemstones come out of the ground, they are called 'rough' gemstones. They may be jagged, dull or stuck in other rocks.

Rough garnet

Rough diamond

From the lab
Synthetic gems do not come from the ground. Chemists make them! They mix elements at the right temperature and pressure.

Cubic zirconia, a lab-created 'diamond'

Rare and **Strange**

Some gemstones are very rare and expensive. Others create special effects.

BLACK OPALS

Opals come in every colour of the rainbow, but black ones are the rarest. Most of them come from one town in Australia: Lightning Ridge.

All opals seem to be flecked with flickering colours.

RARE BEYOND COMPARE

Tanzanite is a rare gemstone that is found in one area of Tanzania, Africa. Painite is another rare gem.

Tanzanite is purply-blue. ▲

Fewer than 100 painite crystals have ever been found! ▲

DOUBLE VISION

Iceland spar is see-through. When you look through it, you see two of everything!

Iceland spar bends and divides light. ◄

Diamonds from space

Some diamonds do not form underground. They fall to Earth from space, inside rocks called meteorites.

Meteorite

COLOUR CHANGE

In sunlight, alexandrite looks green or yellow. In electric light, it looks purple, pink or red.

Alexandrite in natural light ◄

Alexandrite in artificial light ◄

Cutting and
Polishing

Before gemstones are put into jewellery, they are cut and polished. This shows off the stones' colour or sparkle.

▲ A labradorite cabochon

◄ An opal cabochon

COLOURFUL CABOCHON
An opaque gemstone is often cut into a smooth, domed shape called a cabochon. It shows off the gemstone's colours and patterns.

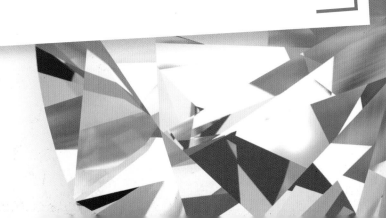

SPARKLING SHAPE

Translucent or see-through gemstones are often cut to have many small, flat windows called facets. These bounce the light around for extra sparkle.

A machine polishes each facet.

Diamonds can be cut into many different, faceted shapes.

Many-sided

The more facets a diamond has, the sparklier it seems. Diamonds can be cut with up to 144 facets.

Famous
Jewels

Gems can make quite a name for themselves – these jewels are world-famous!

MOST FAMOUS

The Crown Jewels belong to the UK's kings and queens. The 13 crowns hold many precious gems. The collection also includes a sceptre decorated with the world's largest cut clear diamond, the Cullinan I.

The Imperial State Crown ▶

Black Prince's Ruby

Cullinan II diamond

RECORD PRICE

In 2016, the Oppenheimer Blue diamond became the most expensive gemstone. It sold for £34,700,000.

The Murat Tiara

This tiara of diamonds and pearls was made as a wedding gift in 1920. In 2012 it sold for £2,400,000.

BIGGEST ROBBERY

One of the world's biggest robberies took place in 2015 in London, UK. The robbers made off with jewels and other loot worth up to £200,000,000.

▼ The robbers blasted open this door to reach the valuables.

ENORMOUS EMERALDS

The world's biggest emeralds come from Brazil's Bahia region. One weighed 341 kg – as much as four men.

An emerald from Bahia, Brazil ▶

Gemstone Guide

AGATE
Type: Mineral
Appearance: Translucent; stripes of colour ranging from white and yellow to blue, red and green

AMBER
Type: Hardened resin
Appearance: Translucent; ranging from yellow to red

AMETHYST
Type: Mineral
Appearance: Transparent to translucent; purple

DIAMOND
Type: Mineral
Appearance: Usually transparent and colourless; may be coloured

EMERALD
Type: Mineral
Appearance: Transparent to translucent; green

JASPER
Type: Mineral
Appearance: Opaque; stripes of brown, yellow, red, green or blue

LAPIS LAZULI
Type: Rock
Appearance: Opaque; blue

OPAL
Type: Similar to a mineral, but not a crystal
Appearance: Transparent to opaque; ranges from white to black, to rainbow colours

RUBY
Type: Mineral
Appearance: Transparent to translucent; red

SAPPHIRE
Type: Mineral
Appearance: Transparent to translucent; usually blue, but may be any colour except red

Glossary

cabochon A polished, rounded gemstone.

crystal The regular shape that a mineral forms as it grows.

element A pure, basic substance.

facet A small, flat surface.

gemstone A beautiful and hard mineral or rock that is used in jewellery.

geode A hollow rock that contains minerals.

iridescent Shimmering with different colours.

meteorite A piece of rock or metal that has fallen to Earth from space.

mineral A solid formed in the ground or in water. Each mineral is a mix of elements.

opaque Not able to be seen through.

pressure A pressing force.

resin A substance that oozes from some trees and other plants.

rock A solid made from different minerals.

translucent Allowing light to pass through, but not able to be seen through clearly.

transparent Able to be seen through clearly.

Index

PICTURE CREDITS

Alamy: 5tr (Zoonar/Aleksandr Volkov), 15bc (NHM, London), 15br (PjrStudio), 17tr (NHM, London), 17cl (Julie Thompson Photography), 17cr (NHM, London), 20 (Granger Historical Picture Archive), 21br (Phil Degginger); **Dreamstime:** 16-17 (Bilalova Indira); **Getty Images:** cover (Doug Armand, impactimage, malerapaso), 1 (malerapaso), 2-3 (miljko), 8-9, (Olivier Polet/Corbis), 15bl (Harry Taylor/DK), 17t (Harry Taylor/DK), 17bct (Harry Taylor/DK), 17bcb (Science Photo Library), 21tl (Fabrice Coffrini/AFP), 21tr (Miguel Medina/AFP), 21bl (Hatton Garden Properties Ltd); **Shutterstock:** 3tr (Reamolko), 4 (J. Palys), 5cl (Albert Russ), 5b (Alexey Lobanov), 6c (Imfoto), 6bl (Rojarin), 6-7 (Imfoto), 7cl (Pisut Phaetrangsee), 7tr (Imfoto), 7cr (Tinalmages), 7cbr (melnikof), 7br (Cutworld), 8 (Sararwut Jaimassiri), 9c (macrowildlife), 9br (David Tadevosian), 10-11 (arka38), 10b (Cagla Acıkgoz), 11tl (verbaska), 11cr (vvoe), 11b (Reload Design), 12 (Simon Zenger), 13tl (lynnette), 13tr (Mivr), 13bl (Bjoern Wylezich), 13br (Priadilshchikova Natalia), 14 (Albert Russ), 15t (Alice Nerr), 18-19 (royaltystockphoto), 18cl (J. Palys), 18bl (ribeiroantonio), 19tr (wideweb), 19br (LifetimeStock), 20-21t (NickKnight), 22tl (arka38), 22clt (humbak), 22cl (Kirill Kurashov), 22clb (LifetimeStock), 22bl (Renu.M), 22tr (ArgenLant), 22crt (Buquet Christophe), 22cr (Tinalmages), 22crb (Rojarin), 22br (Byjeng).